A Note to Parents

For many children, learning math is difficult and "I hate math!" is their first response — to which many parents silently add "Me, too!" Children often see adults comfortably reading and writing, but they rarely have such models for mathematics. And math fear can be catching!

The easy-to-read stories in this **Hello Reader! Math** series were written to give children a positive introduction to mathematics and parents a pleasurable re-acquaintance with a subject that is important to everyone's life. **Hello Reader! Math** stories make mathematical ideas accessible, interesting, and fun for children. The activities and suggestions at the end of each book provide parents with a hands-on approach to help children develop mathematical interest and confidence.

Enjoy the mathematics!
• Give your child a chance to retell the story. The more familiar children are with the story, the more they will understand its mathematical concepts.
• Use the colorful illustrations to help children "hear and see" the math at work in the story.
• Treat the math activities as games to be played for fun. Follow your child's lead. Spend time on those activities that engage your child's interest and curiosity.
• Activities, especially ones using physical materials, help make abstract mathematical ideas concrete.

Learning is a messy process and learning about math calls for children to become immersed in lively experiences that help them make sense of mathematical concepts and symbols.

Although learning about numbers is basic to math, other ideas, such as identifying shapes and patterns, measuring, collecting and interpreting data, reasoning logically, and thinking about chance are also important. By reading these stories and having fun with the activities, you will help your child enthusiastically say **"Hello, math,"** instead of "I hate math."

—Marilyn Burns
National Mathematics Educator
Author of *The I Hate Mathematics! Book*

To Jill
—G.M.

For Paul, a good money manager
—M.H.

Copyright © 1998 by Scholastic Inc.
The activities on pages 27-32 copyright © 1998 by Marilyn Burns.
All rights reserved. Published by Scholastic Inc.
HELLO READER! and CARTWHEEL BOOKS and associated logos
are trademarks and/or registered trademarks of Scholastic Inc.

Library of Congress Cataloging-in-Publication Data
Maccarone, Grace.
    Monster money/by Grace Maccarone; illustrated by Marge Hartelius; math activities by Marilyn Burns.
        p.   cm. — (Hello reader! Math. Level 1)
    Summary: Ten monsters have ten cents apiece to buy a pet in this rhyming story that demonstrates how to count money. Includes math activities.
    ISBN 0-590-12007-7
    [1. Money—Fiction.   2. Counting—Fiction.   3. Monsters—Fiction.
4. Stories in rhyme.]   I. Hartelius, Margaret A., ill.   II. Burns, Marilyn.
III. Title.   IV. Series.
PZ8.3.M127Ms   1998
[E]—dc21
                                                                97-43658
                                                                    CIP
                                                                    AC

10 9 8 7 6 5 4 3 2 1   8 9/9 0/0 01 02

Printed in the U.S.A.   24
First printing, August 1998

Monster Money

by Grace Maccarone
Illustrated by Marge Hartelius
Math Activities by Marilyn Burns

Hello Reader! Math — Level 1

SCHOLASTIC INC.

New York   Toronto   London   Auckland   Sydney

Good morning! Good morning!
Ten cents for a pet,
a monster's best friend.
Which one will you get?

Ten pennies buy a frog.

Ten pennies buy a slug.

Five pennies and one nickel
buy a bug.

Two nickels buy a fly.

Two nickels buy a flea.

One nickel and five pennies
buy a bee.

One dime buys a beetle.

One dime buys a bat.

Five pennies and one nickel
buy a rat.

Ten pennies buy a crab.

Two nickels buy a jellyfish.

One nickel and five pennies
buy a smelly fish.

One dime buys a jiggly thing.

Ten pennies buy a wiggly thing.

Five pennies and one nickel
buy a giggly thing.

Ten cents buy a pet,
a monster's best friend.
Take your pet home
because this is the end!